Superheroes of the Bible

A Devotional & Writing Workbook for Children

SUPERHEROES OF THE BIBLE
A Devotional & Writing Workbook for Children
BY LATE NOVEMBER LEARNING TREE

Published by Late November Literary
Winston Salem, NC 27107

ISBN: 979-8-9988413-3-0

This is a work of nonfiction. Any brand names, places, or trademarks remain the property of their respective owners and are only used for educational purposes.

Library of Congress Cataloging-in-Publication Data:
Late November Learning Tree.
Superheroes of the Bible/ Late November Learning Tree 1st ed.

Printed in the United States of America

HOLY
BIBLE

Mighty Men

Noah

Moses

Caleb & Joshua

Samson

Gideon

Elijah

Elisha

Samuel

Jonathan

David

Eleazar

Daniel

Shadrach, Meshach, and Abednego

Jesus

Peter & John

Paul & Silas

Wonder Women

Miriam

Rahab

Ruth

Deborah & Jael

Hannah

Abigail

Esther

Mary, the mother of Jesus

Priscilla

Lydia

Phoebe

Mighty Men

Noah

Noah lived in a dark world full of sin. God was angry at the sin and told Noah that he would destroy the earth with a big flood. But Noah was the only man who found favor with God, but he needed to follow God's directions if he and his family were to survive the flood. For over 100 years, he built a large ark, following God's specific details. He built it alone with his family while others mocked him. He preached at the crowds telling them that God's judgement was coming, but that they could join him on the ark, but no one listened.

God sent every species of animal to the ark: two of each unclean animal, and seven pairs of the clean animals. That's a lot of animals! But no other human joined the ark outside of Noah and his family. Then God shut the door, and the great flood came. Because Noah obeyed God and honored him, he and his family were saved.

Superhero ability: Obedience, hard worker, preacher

What would you do if God told you to build a big boat because a flood was coming? Do you think anyone would believe you?

What animals would be the coolest to have on the ark? Which ones would cause the most problems? How would you handle it?

How do you imagine Noah?
Draw your own comic strip that tells his superhero story!

Moses

Moses was adopted by Pharoah's daughter and grew up rich. He made a big mistake and hurt someone, so he ran far away. He hid in the desert, hoping no one would find him. But God knew exactly where he was and called out to him from a burning bush!

He told Moses that he was to go back to Egypt and help rescue God's people. Moses said, "How can I do that? I have a speech problem. I can't talk really good." God said, "I'm going with you, and if you do as I say, my people will be free!" Because Moses listened to God, he saw miracles happen before his eyes!

Superhero ability: Obedience and trust in God

What would you do if God started talking to you through a burning bush? What questions would you have for him?

Moses was not confident and didn't think he could lead the people out of bondage. But God was with him. What are you not confident about? What do you need God to help you accomplish?

How do you imagine Moses?
Draw your own comic strip that tells his superhero story!

Samson

Samson's parents wanted their son to take a special vow. This was no ordinary vow. This was a promise made to God, and in return, Samson grew up to be the strongest and most powerful man around. He defeated a thousand men by using a jawbone of a donkey, and his enemies became angrier and angrier because they couldn't find a way to beat him! When Samson broke his promises to God, his strength vanished, and he was overtaken by his enemies and forced to be a slave. Samson called out to God for forgiveness and mercy, and God gave him back his strength and power so that he could defeat all of his enemies one last time.

Superhero ability: Strength, bravery, repentance

What would you do if you were as strong as Samson?

Samson started breaking the promises he made to God, and it cost him his strength. Why is it important we keep our promises?

How do you imagine Samson?

Draw your own comic strip that tells his superhero story!

Gideon

Gideon was the youngest of his family. He was surprised when the angel of the Lord came to him while he was threshing wheat. The angel told him that he was to lead Israel against the enemy that enslaved them and stole all their food. When Gideon made a sacrifice before him, the angel touched it, consumed it, then the angel disappeared. Gideon knew God had spoken to him.

Gideon went and destroyed the altars to other gods and told the people that God would deliver them. But at first, they had too many men. God told Gideon to send them home. Eventually, he was left with only 300 men, but the enemy had over 100,000! Gideon was nervous and asked God for a sign twice! God was patient and showed him that he was with him. With only trumpets, empty jars, and torches, Gideon and his army obeyed God's instructions and watched as God turned the enemy against each other.

Superhero ability: Submission to God, Faith, Courage, Mighty Warrior

How do you imagine Gideon?

Draw your own comic strip that tells his superhero story!

Elijah

Elijah was the only prophet of God left among Israel. There were 450 prophets of Baal, a false god. Elijah was tired of the children of Israel choosing to worship a false god instead of the one true God. He told them to make up their minds! Then he suggested that the 450 prophets of Baal make an altar to their god, and he would make an altar to the one true God. They would each prepare a bull on the altar, but they were not to bring fire to it. Let whichever god was real show himself! Elijah knew that his God would show up in a powerful way. And he did!

The prophets of Baal chanted and danced and cut themselves, but their god did nothing. Elijah soaked his bull and altar in water and even dug a trench around it, filling it with water. Then he prayed! God consumed the whole thing in a powerful fire! The people fell down and worshipped the one true God!

Superhero ability: Prophet, Leader, Fearless, Obedient, Trust in God

Have you ever had to stand up against other people?

Were you nervous? Why should we stand up for God?

Elijah trusted that the one true God would show just how powerful he is. In what ways has God showed you how powerful he is?

How do you imagine Elijah?

Draw your own comic strip that tells his superhero story!

Elisha

Elisha was plowing the ground when the prophet of God, Elijah, passed by and threw his cloak over him. This was a powerful moment where God was transferring his power from one prophet to another. Elisha could have rejected it, but instead, he said good-bye to his family and followed Elijah. He watched as God took Elijah up in a chariot of fire, and his cloak dropped to Elisha. Because he followed God's calling, he continued to lead the children of Israel as a prophet of God. God protected Elisha and blessed him to reach people and continue miracles.

Even when he had died, his bones were still full of the power of God! Some men threw a dead body onto Elisha's bones, and when the body touched the bones, the dead body came back to life!

Superhero ability: Walking in the call of God, submitting to authority, anointed

What would you do if you were Elisha, and someone came and threw their cloak on you, telling you to follow them? In today's times, what would this look like?

Because Elisha obeyed and followed the prophet, God powerfully anointed him, and he helped many people. How do you obey God in your life?

How do you imagine Elisha?

Draw your own comic strip that tells his superhero story!

Caleb & Joshua

Caleb and Joshua were two guys who were chosen among 12 to go and spy on a certain city. This was no ordinary city. This was the place God had promised to Israel. Caleb and Joshua took their job seriously. They were ready to see just how amazing this promised land was. It did not disappoint! There were huge clusters of grapes, and they saw a beautiful land brimming with potential. When they went back to their leader, they were ready to share just how incredible this new land was. But the other 10 spies were cranky and disappointed. They complained and said bad things!

God was pleased that Caleb and Joshua had a good attitude and were focused on positive things, not negative ones. Because they pleased the Lord, they became leaders of Israel and were the only two spies that got to enter and live in that special city.

Superhero ability: Positive attitude, visionary

Have you ever wanted to be a spy? What cool things could you investigate?

God doesn't like it when we are negative and complain. How can we choose to be positive and grateful? Think of something you've complained about. Can you say something positive about it?

How do you imagine Caleb & Joshua?

Draw your own comic strip that tells their superhero story!

Samuel

When Samuel is a young boy, his mom leaves him with a priest to learn the ways of the Lord. One night a voice calls out to him, "Samuel! Samuel!" The boy runs to the priest and says, "Here I am." But it wasn't the priest who called him. After this happened a couple more times, the priest tells Samuel that the Lord is calling him and to answer, "Speak, Lord, for I am listening." Samuel does what he is told, and the Lord speaks about judgement upon the priest and his family. Samuel is scared to tell the priest what the Lord said, but when asked about it, Samuel obeys and shares the message.

Because he obeyed God, he continued to grow in God's favor and eventually becomes a priest to great kings, including King Saul and King David.

Superhero ability: Obedience, leadership

God gives us an important message today to share with others. What is it? Who should we tell about God's message? How can we share his message to them?

How do you imagine Samuel?

Draw your own comic strip that tells his superhero story!

Jonathan

Jonathan was the Prince of Israel, the oldest son of King Saul. He was a fighter and leader, as well as being friendly and Godly. He was also strong and brave. One time, when his father decided not to attack the enemy line, Jonathan and his armor bearer went to handle the situation themselves. They were able to defeat the whole enemy garrison!

Even though he was strong and brave, he was also a friend to David. When Jonathan found out that David had been anointed to be the next king, he didn't get jealous or angry. Instead, he trusted in God and promised David that he would be by his side when the time came for David to be king. The Bible says that he and David loved each other like brothers, and when he died, King David protected Jonathan's family and invited his son to sit at the king's table.

Superhero ability: Loyalty, warrior, humble, good friend

What would it be like to be a prince with a powerful king as your father?

Jonathan was good friends with David. What does it mean to be a good friend?

How do you imagine Jonathan?

Draw your own comic strip that tells his superhero story!

David

David was a shepherd, a musician, a warrior, and eventually a king. When he was a boy shepherd, the prophet Samuel poured a horn of oil over him, declaring him the next king. Yet, he stayed a shepherd for years after that. He wasn't even allowed to join the army and fight, even though there was a giant warrior threatening all of Israel. But David had strong faith in God, and he wasn't afraid. The time came for him to deliver food to his older brothers who were in the army. When David saw that no one was brave enough to fight the giant warrior, Goliath, David immediately volunteered.

After he faced and killed the giant, David grew in popularity. He fought many battles and won all of them. The crowds loved him, which made King Saul go crazy in jealousy. The king decided he must kill David at once. But instead of David growing bitter and angry, he continued to pray and write psalms to the Lord. He believed God would turn it around for good, and that's eventually what happened.

Superhero ability: Strength, fighter, worshipper, leader

What "giants" are in people's lives today? Why is it important that we are not afraid of these "giants" but to trust in the Lord instead?

If you could meet David, what would you say to him? What would you want to know? Would you give him any tips or advice?

How do you imagine David?

Draw your own comic strip that tells his superhero story!

Eleazar

Eleazar was one of King David's "Mighty Men." He and David were good friends and fought closely together in many battles.

One major victory happened when the enemy attacked Israel's troops in Pas-dammim. All of Israel's soldiers fell back and ran away from the battle, but not Eleazar. He and David fought side-by-side, and together, they defeated the entire enemy army! Eleazar fought so hard his hand was frozen around his sword.

Superhero ability: Courage, strength, loyalty

How would you fight off an entire army with just you and your best friend? Would you run like others, or would you stay and fight?

What "enemies" do we face today, and why is it important that we don't give up? What can we learn from Eleazar's story?

How do you imagine Eleazar?

Draw your own comic strip that tells his superhero story!

Daniel

Daniel loved God and prayed three times a day. He was also a friend of the Persian King Darius. There were some of the king's men who were jealous of Daniel and his friendship with the king. They decided they would trick the king into signing a decree that there could be no praying to any other god, and all the people must only worship the king. This distressed Daniel, but he refused to stop praying to God.

The jealous men caught him and dragged him to King Darius. They demanded he be thrown into a den full of hungry lions. The king was upset, but he had no choice but to follow his decree. The next morning, he went to check on his friend, Daniel, and sure enough, Daniel was still alive! God had sent an angel to shut the mouths of the lions and protect Daniel from their attack.

Superhero ability: Prayer warrior, faithful to God, lion tamer

What would you do if you were thrown into a lion's den?

What would be your plan to survive?

____

____

____

____

____

____

____

Daniel prayed three times a day and kept praying even when he knew he'd get in trouble. Do you pray? Would you keep praying even if you knew you'd get in trouble?

How do you imagine Daniel?

Draw your own comic strip that tells his superhero story!

The 3 Hebrew Boys

Shadrach, Meshach, and Abednego were three Hebrew boys that served King Nebuchadnezzar. The king liked the boys, but what he liked even more was when his kingdom worshipped him. He decided to build a great big statue of himself and order everyone to bow and worship the statue whenever they heard the music play. But the Hebrew boys only worshipped the one true God. When the statue was finished, and the music began to play, everyone bowed to the idol, but not the three Hebrew boys. The king became very angry and ordered them to bow or be thrown in a furnace of fire. When they still refused to bow to the idol, the king ordered the furnace be made as hot as it could be and then they threw the three Hebrew boys into it to burn. Yet, that's not what happened! When the king looked into the furnace to see what happened, he saw four in the fire...not three! None of the Hebrew boys died that day. They pulled them out of the fire in awe that the God they served had protected them.

Superhero ability: Faith, bravery, determination, firefighters

What would you do if you were forced to bow before an idol? Would you be brave even if it meant being thrown in fire?

What does standing for our faith look like today? It might not mean being thrown into fire, but how does it still require courage?

How do you imagine the three Hebrew boys?

Draw your own comic strip that tells their superhero story!

Jesus

Jesus was not only the mightiest of all, he was also the Son of God! Yet, he didn't want a throne or to be in a palace. He wanted to heal people and love them. He wanted to show people a better way. When he knew the time was coming for him to die a horrible death on a cross, he went to a garden to pray. He asked God the father to "take this cup" from him, but yet, "nevertheless your will, not mine." Even though he knew what pain and torture waited for him, he went to it willingly because that was the only way his people could be with him forever in heaven. After he died on the cross, Jesus rose from the dead. He did the ultimate miracle; he beat death and hell and gave all of us hope to live with him one day!

Superhero ability: Perfect, humble, all-loving, all-powerful, defeated death

Read:

How can we love others like Jesus loves us? How else can we be more like Jesus?

When the Bible says "take up our cross" to follow Jesus, that implies sacrifices need to be made. What sacrifices in our lives need to be made to serve others like Jesus did?

How do you imagine Jesus performing miracles?

Draw your own comic strip that tells his superhero story!

Peter & John

Peter and John were helping spread the word about Jesus being resurrected from the dead! Many were added to the church. One day, on the way to the temple, a lame man was begging for coins. Peter said to the sick man, "I don't have any money, but I do have something that can help you! In the name of Jesus Christ, rise up and walk!" The lame man stood up and was miraculously healed! He was so excited he started running and shouting and worshipping the Lord. So much so that it got Peter and John in trouble. But they didn't stop spreading the gospel! They told everyone they could. Even when they were beaten and thrown in jail, they didn't stop telling others about Jesus.

Superhero ability: Faith, power, preaching

What are ways we can help the poor?

How were Peter and John bold in their faith? How can you be bold in your faith today? What can you do for others that show them the power of Jesus?

How do you imagine Peter & John?

Draw your own comic strip that tells their superhero story!

Paul & Silas

Paul and Silas got in trouble for preaching the gospel. They were thrown in jail and were put in chains so that they couldn't escape. Instead of feeling bad and complaining, Paul and Silas began to sing and worship the Lord. They worshipped through the whole night! Suddenly, there was an earthquake, and their chains fell off and the jail doors were thrown open wide! Everyone got to escape. The jailer was scared and was going to hurt himself, but Paul and Silas stopped him and told him about Jesus. The jailer got saved that night, and Paul and Silas were freed!

Superhero ability: worshippers, preaching, escape artists

What would you have done if you were thrown in jail for telling others about Jesus?

Paul & Silas worshipped God with songs while in jail, and it made a big difference! Why are songs and worship so important in our lives today? Why should we be careful with songs we listen to and sing?

How do you imagine Paul & Silas?

Draw your own comic strip that tells their superhero story!

Wonder Women

Miriam

Miriam was Moses's older sister. When the little baby boys were going to be killed, their mother wrapped Moses up and placed him in a basket, hoping that an Egyptian would find him and raise him. Miriam loved her baby brother and kept watch over Moses to make sure he was safe and found. When Pharaoh's daughter found little Moses in the basket, she decided to raise him as her son! He would be raised in the Pharoah's palace! Miriam was brave and approached Pharaoh's daughter, telling her about a woman who could care for the baby. Pharoah's daughter ended up using Moses's mother to raise him and take care of him! When Moses eventually led the children of Israel out of Egypt and to freedom, Miriam was still there, supporting her brother and helping him any chance she could.

Superhero ability: Protector, bravery, helper

Do you have a brother or sister or maybe a cousin? Do you get along or do you fight? How can you support each other like Miriam supported Moses?

Miriam watched for years as her little brother grew up in a palace while she was still a slave. Would that make you jealous? What would it be like living in a palace versus living as a slave?

How do you imagine Miriam?
Draw your own comic strip that tells her superhero story!

Rahab

Rahab's life was far from perfect. She lived in Jericho and was an outcast. When a couple of Israel's spies needed a place to hide, they knocked on Rahab's door and asked for help. She knew they were different and weren't from Jericho. She knew that she would get in serious trouble for hiding foreign spies. But she was brave and let them hide in her house. When the authorities were looking for them, she hid them on the roof and helped them escape. She asked that they remember her and her family if their armies were to ever attack Jericho. They said they would remember her protecting them and helping them escape. When the children of Israel came to march around Jericho, the spies remembered Rahab, and she and her house were spared from any attack. She became the great-great grandmother of King David, and Jesus came from her lineage too! All because she chose to do what was right in a time of conflict.

Superhero ability: Protector, helper, valiant woman

What would you do if spies knocked on your door and asked if you could help them hide?

Because Rahab did the right thing, she was protected when the spies brought their army. How does doing the right thing in our lives today "protect" us?

____

____

____

____

____

____

____

How do you imagine Rahab?

Draw your own comic strip that tells her superhero story!

Ruth

When Ruth was a young woman, her husband died. She didn't know what to do, so she followed his mother, Naomi, back to Israel to live with their people. They were so poor that Ruth would go and pick up whatever was leftover from the harvesters in the fields. But she kept a good attitude, vowing to serve the one true God and to helping Naomi. When she caught the eye of the owner of the field, Boaz, he ordered for more grain to be left purposefully for her. Because of her hard work and determination to work the fields every day, she and Boaz eventually fell in love and married.

This young woman from another country may have become a widow, but God saw her positive attitude and continued hard work and made her prosper.

Superhero ability: Positive attitude, hard-working, responsible

Why is having a positive attitude—even when life gets hard—so important? Have you ever caught yourself complaining? How can you make your attitude more positive?

How do you imagine Ruth?

Draw your own comic strip that tells her superhero story!

Deborah & Jael

These two women, Deborah & Jael, lived during the same time and were fierce in their defense of Israel and in making decisions that led their people to victory! Deborah was a prophet and a judge during a time when her people were being held captive by the evil king of Canaan. She told Israel's captain that God would deliver Israel from the enemy and to go and claim victory. When he acted unsure and asked if she would go with them, she said yes, but because he acted unsure, the victory would come through a woman! That's where Jael comes into the picture! All of the enemy were defeated other than the mean captain, Sisera. He found a tent with a woman in it, named Jael. She said to come in, and she got him something to drink. When he was fast asleep, she used a tent peg to drive through his temple, ultimately leading to complete victory of the enemy! Because of both of these women, Israel was free!

Superhero abilities: Strength, fearless, powerful, courageous

What would you do if God wanted you to be a leader of his people? What if he asked you to do hard things?

What would you do if an enemy soldier asked to hide in your tent? In what ways could you be brave, like Jael?

How do you imagine Deborah & Jael?

Draw your own comic strip that tells their superhero story!

Hannah

Hannah was a young woman who had a good life. She had a loving husband, and he took care of her. What she didn't have was a child of her own. Year after year, she prayed and prayed, believing that God would one day hear her prayers and answer her with a child. One day, she traveled to the temple and began weeping before God, earnestly asking him to answer her prayer. The priest saw her and came to her, telling her that God would answer her prayer! She vowed that if God gave her a son, she would give the child back to God to serve his people. The next year, God had answered her prayer, and she had a son named Samuel. Because God honored her, she honored him and gave Samuel to the Lord to serve his people. Samuel grew up to be a great prophet, and because Hannah honored her promise to God, she had many other children.

Superhero ability: Prayer warrior, faithful, honorable

Have you ever wanted something so bad that it made you sad to think about?

The priest told Hannah that God had heard her prayer, and God answered it! Do you believe that God hears your prayers? Do you believe he can do anything, like he did with Hannah?

How do you imagine Hannah?

Draw your own comic strip that tells her superhero story!

Abigail

Abigail was married to a mean man. He refused to help David and his men when they needed food and supplies. Abigail saw that it angered David, and that they were in trouble if her husband didn't change his mind! She followed David and his men and brought them food and provision, which helped David not be so angry. She asked forgiveness and prayed that God would bless David as king when the time came. Because of her quick thinking, she spared her husband and all of the servants who worked for him. David commended her saying that she stopped much bloodshed and that they would leave in peace.

When Abigail's husband died a few days later from a heart attack, and David heard, he requested that the beautiful, quick-thinking Abigail become his wife.

Superhero ability: Quick thinking, peacemaker, smart and kind

What would you do if someone close to you did a bad thing, and it got other people upset? Would you help them fix it, or would you let them be punished?

Abigail had to think fast, and because she was quick-thinking, she calmed down David and his men. In what ways have you seen quick-thinking work to help a situation?

How do you imagine Abigail?
Draw your own comic strip that tells her superhero story!

Esther

Esther was a beautiful Jewish girl raised by her uncle, Mordechai. When she was found by the king's men, she was chosen to marry King Xerxes of Persia and become queen. When she uncovered a secret plot from the king's right-hand man, which would kill all of the Jewish people in the kingdom, she was scared and didn't know what to do. Mordechai encouraged her to go to the king and to tell him of the secret plot or all of her people would die. Esther knew that she could never approach the king without an invitation first, but she pushed back her fear and bravely said, "If I perish, I perish." She went before the king, and he was so overcome by her beauty and bravery that he listened to her.

When he found out his right-hand man had tricked him in signing a wrongful order, King Xerxes commanded his right-hand man to be punished for such deception, and the Jewish people were saved.

Superhero ability: Bravery, loyalty, faithfulness, quick-thinking

Have you ever had to do something that made you really nervous? How did you overcome being so nervous?

What would you do if you had that kind of power like King Xerxes? How would you use your power for good? Would you want people being scared to approach you?

How do you imagine Esther?
Draw your own comic strip that tells her superhero story!

Mary

Mary was a Jewish girl from a humble town called Nazareth. A young man named Joseph was interested in marrying her. The angel, Gabriel, visited Mary and told her that she was highly favored of God and that God had chosen her to be the mother of his son. Mary was shocked! She wasn't even married yet, and she probably wondered if she was even ready to be a mother! But she had faith and trusted in God, saying, "Be it unto me according to thy word."
There were those who didn't understand and mocked her and talked about her behind her back. Joseph was upset and wanted to end their relationship, but the angel spoke to Joseph too and told him that everything that happened was of God. Thankfully, Joseph did the right thing and stayed by Mary's side, even helping her deliver the Son of God.

Superhero ability: Faith and trust, submission, mothering the Messiah

God asks some crazy things of his people. What is something God wants you to do, but you're worried about what others might think? Will you do it anyway?

Mary was probably very scared, but the angel told her to "Fear not." Have you ever been truly scared? Why is it important that we overcome our fear by turning to God?

____

____

____

____

____

____

____

How do you imagine Mary?

Draw your own comic strip that tells her superhero story!

Priscilla

Priscilla and her husband, Aquila, were tentmakers, along with Paul. They travelled with him as missionaries and supported the cause of the gospel. But Priscilla was special in that she not only helped her husband as a tentmaker, she was also a teacher, mentoring a young man who would eventually become a preacher in his own right. She is mentioned several times as a woman who worked hard, taught and mentored others, and even risked her life for the cause of Christ.

She shows the strength of women as leaders, taking care of her family and others, all while teaching and helping others know Jesus.

Superhero ability: Teacher, mentor, tentmaker, missionary and leader

Priscilla was a strong, leading woman. Do you know a strong, leading woman? Describe who this woman is to you and what makes her so strong.

____

____

____

____

____

____

____

Priscilla helped her husband with tentmaking, but she was also a teacher and mentor. Why is important to have good teachers? Who have been good teachers to you?

How do you imagine Priscilla?

Draw your own comic strip that tells her superhero story!

Lydia

Lydia was a smart and wealthy woman who is the first recorded European to become a Christian. She was "a dealer of purple," which means she was important in the marketplace where purple dyes and cloths were very expensive. She listened to a sermon from Paul when he travelled to Philippi, and she was baptized into the faith. She poured herself into helping Paul and the other missionaries, inviting them into her home and providing them food and shelter so that they could continue preaching the gospel.

Because of her willingness to accept Christ and help the missionaries, more people in European countries were able to hear the gospel.

Superhero ability: a good listener, a hard worker, generous and resourceful

The rich wore purple back in the Bible days. What do people wear or own to show wealth today?

Lydia helped in little, everyday ways. She provided food, shelter, resources, but she probably didn't think anything of it. Why are little things sometimes big things in Jesus's eyes? What little things can you do for others?

How do you imagine Lydia?

Draw your own comic strip that tells her superhero story!

Phoebe

Phoebe is only mentioned one time in the Bible! We don't know her age or if she was ever married, but that doesn't make her less of a superhero!

Paul said a lot about her in Romans 16. She was a "deacon" in the ministry, which means she held a position of leadership in the church. Not only that, but she was a "benefactor" to Paul and other missionaries, which means she provided funds and resources to help them travel. What's even cooler than all of that is that Paul trusted her to carry the letter of Romans to the Romans church, telling them to honor her for good services to the church and because of her leadership.

Superhero ability: Church leadership, messenger of the Romans epistle, helper

How important were "letter carriers" back in the Bible times before technology, cars, and airplanes? What does it say about Phoebe that Paul trusted her to accomplish the message delivery?

Women were not treated as equals as men in the Bible times. But God is "no respecter of person." Why is important that we treat each other with respect and honor, regardless of if we are men or women?

How do you imagine Phoebe?

Draw your own comic strip that tells her superhero story!

Thank you for supporting

Late November Learning Tree!

Consider our other educational workbooks:

Sight Words

Journaling for Kids

Journaling Is Writing Too!

Journaling through Scripture

Paragraph Practice

Essay Writing

...and more!

Visit us at www.latenovemberliterary.com